THE GNOSTIC CRUCIFIXION

G.R.S. Mead

ECHOES FROM THE GNOSIS.

Under this general title is now being published a series of small volumes, drawn from, or based upon, the mystic, theosophic and gnostic writings of the ancients, so as to make more easily audible for the ever-widening circle of those who love such things, some echoes of the mystic experiences and initiatory lore of their spiritual ancestry. There are many who love the life of the spirit, and who long for the light of gnostic illumination, but who are not sufficiently equipped to study the writings of the ancients at first hand, or to follow unaided the labours of scholars. These little volumes are therefore intended to serve as introduction to the study of the more difficult literature of the subject; and it is hoped that at the same time they may become for some, who have, as yet, not even heard of the Gnosis, stepping-stones to higher things.

G. R. S. M.

CONTENTS

PREFACE.

The Gnostic Mystery of the Crucifixion is most clearly set forth in the new-found fragments of *The Acts of John,* and follows immediately on the Sacred Dance and Ritual of Initiation which we endeavoured to elucidate in Vol. IV. of these little books, in treating of *The Hymn of Jesus.*

The reader is, therefore, referred to the "Preamble" of that volume for a short introduction concerning the nature of the Gnostic Acts in general and of the Leucian *Acts of John* in particular. I would, however, add a point of interest bearing on the date which was forgotten, though I have frequently remarked upon it when lecturing on the subject.

The strongest proof that we have in our fragment very early material is found in the text itself, when it relates the following simple form of the miracle of the loaves.

"Now if at any time He were invited by one of the Pharisees and went to the bidding, we used to go with Him. And before each was set a single loaf by the host; and of them He Himself also received one. Then He would give thanks and divide His loaf among us; and from this little each had enough, and our own loaves were saved whole, so that those who bade Him were amazed."

If the marvellous narratives of the feeding of the five thousand had been already in circulation, it is incredible that this simple story, which we may so easily believe, should have been invented. Of what use, when the minds of the hearers had been strung to the pitch of faith which had already accepted the feeding of the five thousand as an actual physical occurrence, would it have been to invent comparatively so small a wonder? On the other hand, it is easy to believe that from similar simple stories of the power of the Master, which were first of all circulated in the inner circles, the popular narratives of the multitude-feeding miracles could be developed. We, therefore, conclude, with every probability, that we have here an indication of material of very early date.

Nevertheless when we come to the Mystery of the Crucifixion as set forth in our fragment, we are not entitled to argue that the popular history was developed from it in a similar fashion. The problem it raises is of another order, and to it we will return when the reader has been put in possession of the narrative, as translated from Bonnet's text. John is supposed to be the narrator.

(The Arabic figures and the Roman figures in square brackets refer respectively to Bonnet's and James' texts. I have added the side figures for convenience of reference in the comments.)

THE VISION OF THE CROSS.

1. And having danced these things with us, Beloved, the Lord went out. And we, as though beside ourselves, or wakened out of sleep, fled each our several ways.

2. I, however, though I saw the beginning of His passion could not stay to the end, but fled unto the Mount of Olives weeping over that which had befallen.

3. And when He was hung on the tree of the cross, at the sixth hour of the day darkness came over the whole earth.

And my Lord stood in the midst of the Cave, and filled it with light, and said:

4. "John, to the multitude below, in Jerusalem, I am being crucified, and pierced with spears and reeds, and vinegar and gall is being given Me to drink. To thee now I speak, and give ear to what I say. 'Twas I who put it in thy heart to ascend this Mount, that thou mightest hear what disciple should learn from Master, and man from God."

5. And having thus spoken, He showed me a Cross of Light set up, and round the Cross a vast multitude, and therein one form and a similar appearance, and in the Cross another multitude not having one form.

6. And I beheld the Lord Himself above the Cross. He had, however, no shape, but only as it were a voice—

not, however, this voice to which we are accustomed, but one of its own kind and beneficent and truly of God, saying unto me:

7. "John, one there needs must be to hear those things, from Me; for I long for one who will hear.

8. "This Cross of Light is called by Me for your sakes sometimes Word (Logos), sometimes Mind, sometimes Jesus, sometimes Christ, sometimes Door, sometimes Way, sometimes Bread, sometimes Seed, sometimes Resurrection, sometimes Son, sometimes Father, sometimes Spirit, sometimes Life, sometimes Truth, sometimes Faith, sometimes Grace.

9. "Now those things [it is called] as towards men; but as to what it is in truth, itself in its own meaning to itself, and declared unto Us, [it is] the defining (or delimitation) of all things, both the firm necessity of things fixed from things unstable, and the 'harmony' of Wisdom.

10. "And as it is Wisdom in 'harmony,' there are those on the Right and those on the Left—powers, authorities, principalities, and dæmons, energies, threats, powers of wrath, slanderings—and the Lower Root from which hath come forth the things in genesis.

11. "This, then, is the Cross which by the Word (Logos) hath been the means of 'cross-beaming' all things—at the same time separating off the things that

proceed from genesis and those below it [from those above], and also compacting them all into one.

12. "But this is not the cross of wood which thou shalt see when thou descendest hence; nor am I he that is upon the cross—[I] whom now thou seest not, but only hearest a voice.

13. "I was held [to be] what I am not, not being what I was to many others; nay, they will call Me something else, abject and not worthy of Me. As, then, the Place of Rest is neither seen nor spoken of, much more shall I, the Lord of it, be neither seen [nor spoken of].

14. "Now the multitude of one appearance round the Cross is the Lower Nature. And as to those whom thou seest in the Cross, if they have not also one form, [it is because] the whole Race (or every Limb) of Him who descended hath not yet been gathered together.

15. "But when the Upper Nature, yea, the Race that is coming unto Me, in obedience to My Voice, is taken up, then thou who now hearkenest to Me, shalt become it, and it shall no longer be what it is now, but above them as I am now.

16. "For so long as thou callest not thyself Mine, I am not what I am. But if thou hearkenest unto Me, hearing, thou, too, shalt be as I [am], and I shall be what I was, when thou [art] as I am with Myself; for from this thou art.

17. "Pay no attention, then, to the many, and them that are without the mystery think little of; for know that I am wholly with the Father and the Father with Me.

18. "Nothing, then, of the things which they will say of Me have I suffered; nay that Passion as well which I showed unto thee and the rest, by dancing [it], I will that it be called a mystery.

19. "What thou art, thou seest; this did I show unto thee. But what I am, this I alone know, [and] none else.

20. "What, then, is Mine suffer Me to keep; but what is thine see thou through Me. To see Me as I really am I said is not possible, but only what thou art able to recognise, as being kin [to Me] (or of the same Race).

21. "Thou hearest that I suffered; yet I did not suffer: that I suffered not; yet I did suffer: that I was pierced; yet was I not smitten: that I was hanged; yet I was not hanged: that blood flowed from me; yet it did not flow: and in a word the things they say about Me I had not, and the things they do not say those I suffered. Now what they are I will riddle for thee; for I know that thou wilt understand.

22. "Understand, therefore, in Me, the slaying of a Word (Logos), the piercing of a Word, the blood of a Word, the wounding of a Word, the hanging of a Word, the passion of a Word, the nailing (or putting together) of a Word, the death of a Word.

23. "And thus I speak separating off the man. First, then, understand the Word, then shalt thou understand the Lord, and in the third place [only] the man and what he suffered."

24. And having said these things to me, and others which I know not how to say as He Himself would have it, He was taken up, no one of the multitude beholding Him.

25. And when I descended I laughed at them all, when they told Me what they did concerning Him, firmly possessed in myself of this [truth] only, that the Lord contrived all things symbolically, and according to [His] dispensation for the conversion and salvation of man.

COMMENTS.

The translation is frequently a matter of difficulty, for the text has been copied in a most careless and unintelligent fashion, so that the ingenuity of the editors has often been taxed to the utmost and has not infrequently completely broken down. It is of course quite natural that orthodox scribes should blunder when transcribing Gnostic documents, owing to their ignorance of the subject and their strangeness to the ideas; but this particular copyist is at times quite barbarous, and as the subject is deeply mystical and deals with the unexpected, the reconstruction of the original reading is a matter of great difficulty. With a number of passages I am still unsatisfied, though I hope they are somewhat nearer the spirit of the original than other reconstructions which have been attempted.

It is always a matter of difficulty for the rigidly objective mind to understand the point of view of the Gnostic scripture-writers. One thing, however, is certain: they lived in times when the rigid orthodoxy of the canon was not yet established. They were in the closest touch with the living tradition of scripture-writing, and they knew the manner of it.

The probability is that paragraphs 1-3 are from the pen of the redactor or compiler of the *Acts*, and that the narrative, beginning with the words "And my Lord stood in the midst of the Cave," is incorporated from prior material—a mystic vision or apocalypse circulated in the inner circles.

The compiler knows the general Gospel-story, and seems prepared to admit its historical basis; at the same time he knows well that the story circulated among the people is but the outer veil of the mystery, and so he hands on what we may well believe was but one of many visions of the mystic crucifixion.

The gentle contempt of those who had entered into the mystery, for those unknowing ones who would fain limit the crucifixion to one brief historic event, is brought out strongly, and savours, though mildly, of the bitterness of the struggle between the two great forces of the inner and spiritualizing and the outer and materializing traditions.

I. The disciples flee after beholding the inner mystery of the Passion and At-one-ment as set forth in the initiating drama of the Mystic Dance which formed the subject of our fourth volume.

2. Yet even John the Beloved, in spite of this initiation, cannot yet bear the thought that his Master did actually suffer historically as a malefactor on the physical cross. In his distress he flees unto the Mount of Olives, above Jerusalem.

But to the Gnostic the Mount of Olives was no physical hill, though it was a mount in the physical, and Jerusalem no physical city, though a city in the physical.

The Mount, however it might be distinguished locally, was the Height of Contemplation, and the bringing into activity of a certain inner consciousness; even as Jerusalem here was the Jerusalem below, the physical consciousness.

3. The sentence "when He was hung on the tree of the Cross" contains a great puzzle. The word for "tree" in the original is *batos*; this may mean the "bush" or "tree" of the cross. But the Cross for the Gnostics was a living symbol. It was not only the cross of dead wood, or the dead trunk of a tree lopped of its branches—a symbol of Osiris in death; it was also the Tree of Life, and was equated with the "Fiery Bush" out of which the Angel of God spake to Moses—that is the Tree of Fiery Life, in the Paradise of man's inner nature, whence the Word of God expresses itself to one who is worthy to hear. And this Tree of Life was also, as the Cross, the Tree of Knowledge of Good and Evil; indeed, both are but one Tree, for the fruit of the Tree of Life is the knowledge of good and evil, the cross of the opposites.

But seeing that the word *batos* in Greek had also another meaning, the Gnostics, by their method of mystical word-play, based on the power of sound, brought this further meaning into use for the expansion of the idea. The difference of accentuation and of gender (though the reading of the Septuagint is masculine and not feminine as is usual with *batos* in the sense of bush or tree) presented no difficulty to the word-alchemy of these allegorists.

Hippolytus, in his *Refutation of all Heretics*, attempts to summarize a system of the Christianized Gnosis which is assigned to the Docetæ; and Docetism is precisely the chief characteristic of our *Acts of John*, as we have already pointed out in Vol. IV. In this unsympathetic summary there is a passage which throws some light on our puzzle. It would, of course, require a detailed analysis of our hæresiologist's "refutation" of the Docetic system to make the passage to which we refer[1] fully comprehensible; but as this would be too lengthy an undertaking for these short comments, we must content ourselves with a bald statement.

The pure spiritual emanations or ideas or intelligences of the Light descend into the lowest Darkness of matter. For the moulding of vehicles or bodies for them it is necessary to call in the aid of the God of Fire, the creative or rather formative Power, who is "Living Fire begotten of Light."

Hippolytus summarizes, doubtless imperfectly, from the Docetic document that lay before him, as follows:

"Moses refers to this God as the Fiery God who spake from the *Batos*, that is to say, from the Dark Air; for *Batos* is all the Air subjected to Darkness."

That is, presumably, the material Air, Air of the Darkness, as compared with the spiritual Air or Air of

---

[1] *op. cit.*, viii., 9

the Light. The Docetic writer, Hippolytus says, explained the use of the term as follows:

"Moses called it *Batos*, because, in their passing from Above, Below, all the Ideas of the Light [that is, the Light-sparks or spirits of men] used the Air as their means of passage (*batos*)."

In other words *Batos*, as Air, was the link between Light and Darkness, which Darkness was regarded as essentially a flowing or Watery chaos. The Batos was the Way Down and the Way Up of souls.

We are not, however, to suppose that the origin of this idea was the text of *Exodus*. By no means; the idea came first, indeed was fundamental with the Gnosis; the mystic exegesis of the "burning bush" passage was an exercise in ingenuity. For the Gnosis, the that which at once separated and united the Light and the Darkness was the Cross. The Angel of God speaking to Moses out of the Fiery Batos was for the Christian Gnostics one of the most striking apocalypses of ancient Jewish scripture; and it was primarily one of the chief functions of the Gnosis to throw light on the under-meaning. This the Docetic exegete does in his own fashion, using the reading of the Greek Targum or Translation of the Seventy, in this wise: "*Batos? Batos* does not mean 'bush' really, but 'medium of transmission,'" It is by means of this that the Word of God comes unto us—namely, by the mystery of the uniter-separator in one, which was called by many names.

For instance, in setting forth the Sophia-mythus, or Wisdom-story, or mystery of cosmogenesis, of the Valentinian school, Hippolytus[2], treats of the Cross as the final mystery of all. With original documents before him, he writes:

"Now it is called Boundary, because it bounds off the Deficiency from the Fullness [so as to make it] exterior to it; it is called Partaker because it partakes of the Deficiency as well; and it is called Cross (or Stock) because it hath been fixed immovably and unchangeably, so that nothing of the Deficiency should be able to approach the eternities within the Fullness."

Here it is useless to tie oneself to the physical symbol of a cross. The Stauros (Cross) in its true self is a living idea, a reality or root-principle. It is the principle of separation and limit, dividing entity from non-entity, being from non-being, perfection from imperfection, fullness or sufficiency from deficiency or insufficiency—Light from Darkness. It is the that which causes all opposites. At the same time it shares in all opposites, for it is the immediate emanation of the Father Himself, and therefore unites while separating. It is, therefore, the principle of participation or sharing in, sharing in both the Fullness and the Deficiency. Finally, it is the Stock or Pillar as that which "has stood, stands and will stand"—the principle of immobility, as the energy of the Father in His aspect of the supreme

---

[2] *op. cit.,* vi. 3

Individuality that changes not, because he is Lord of the ever-changing.

That such a master-idea is difficult to grasp goes without saying; it was confessedly the supreme mystery. From it the mind, the formal mind of man, "falls back unable to grasp it"; for it is precisely this personal mind that creates duality, and insinuates itself between cause and effect. The spiritual Mind alone can embrace the opposites.

But to return to our text. "When He was hung on the *batos* of the Cross"—when He had reached the state of balance, was in the mystic centre—then at the sixth hour, that is mid-day, when there was greatest light, there was also greatest darkness.

And then when the Lord, the Higher Self of the man, was balanced and justified, the man, the disciple, became conscious, in the cave of his heart—that is to say, in his inmost substantial nature—of the Presence of Light.

4. Thereon follow the illumination and the explanation of the familiar drama of appearance taught to those "without the mystery."

"The multitude below in Jerusalem" is the lower nature of the man, his unillumined mind. "Jerusalem Below" is set over against "Jerusalem Above," the City of God. Jerusalem Below is that nature in him that is still unordered and unpurified; while Jerusalem Above is that ordered and purified portion of his substance that can respond to the immediate shining of the Light, which further orders it according to the Ordering of Heaven.

And yet the drama below is real enough; there are ever crucifixion and piercing and the drinking of vinegar and gall, before the triumphant Christ is born. It is by such means that His Body is conformed; it is the mystery of the transformation of what we call evil into good. The Body of the Christ is perfected by the absorption of the impersonal evil of the world, which He transmutes into blessing.

"'Twas I who put it in thy heart to ascend this Mount." I am thy Self, thy true God; 'twas I energizing in thee who enabled thee to rise to the height of contemplation, where thou canst "hear what disciple should learn from Master and man from God." The man has now reached the stage of Hearer in the Spiritual Mysteries.

5. There then follows the vision of the great Cross of Light, fixed firm, and stretching from earth to heaven. Round its foot on earth is a vast multitude of all the nations of the world; they resemble one another in that they are configured according to the Darkness, their "Spark burns low." On the Cross, or in it, for doubtless the seer saw within as well as without, was another multitude of various grades of light, being formed into some marvellous Image like unto the Divine, but not yet completed—as it might be the Rose on the Cross, in the famous symbol of the Rosicrucians.

6. And above the Cross, lost in the dazzling brilliancy of the Fullness, John beheld the Lord; he *beheld* but could not *see*, because of the Great Light, as we are told in another great vision of the Master in the *Pistis Sophia*. He can hear only a Voice. But this Voice is no voice of man, but one "truly of God"—a Bath-kol or "Heavenly Voice," as the Rabbis called it—a Voice of sweetest reasonableness, using no words, but of a higher order of utterance, that can make the man speak to himself in his own language, using his own terms.

7. The sentence "I long for one who will hear," is instinct with the yearning of the Divine Love, the eagerness to bestow, the longing to speak if only there be one to hear.

8. There then follows a list of synonyms of the Cross, every one of which shows that the Cross, if a symbol, must be taken to denote the master-symbol of all symbols. It is the key to the chief nomenclature of the Gnosis and the greatest terms of the Gospel. These terms, it is stated, are used by the Wisdom "for your sakes," that is, to bring home in many ways to the hearts of men the intuition of the mystery.

As is explained later on in the text, the mystery of the Cross is the mystery of the Word, the Spiritual Man, or Great Man, the Divine Individuality. Therefore is it called Word or Reason, Mind, Jesus and Christ. Son and Father; for Jesus is the Christ, both as human and divine, the two natures uniting in one in the Cross; and the Son is the Father in a still more divine meaning of the mystery; for both Son and Cross are of the Father alone, they are Himself manifesting Himself to Himself. The whole is the mystery of Ātman or the Self.

The Door is the Door of the Two in One, the state of equilibrium of the opposites which opens out into the all-embracing consciousness and understanding of all oppositions.

The Cross is the Way on which there is no travelling, for it perpetually enters into itself; it is the true Method, not so much in the sense of the Way-between or the Medium or Mediator, as in the sense of the Means of Gnosis.

It is also called Seed because it is the mystery of the power of growth and development; it is self-initiative.

And if the Cross be Son and Father in separation and union, or as simultaneously Cause and Result, it is likewise Spirit or Ātman, and therefore Life.

It is also Truth or the Perpetual Paradox, distinguishing and uniting in itself all pros and cons, and all analysis and synthesis in simultaneous operation.

Therefore also is it called Faith, because it is the that which is stable and unchanging amid perpetual change. Faith in its true mystic meaning seems to denote the power of withdrawing the personal consciousness from between the pairs of opposites, where these appear external and other than oneself, and embracing the opposites within the greater consciousness, when they are within oneself and appear as natural processes in the great economy.

Faith is of the contemplative mind; it embraces, it includes. It is therefore of the Great Mother, as the life and substance of the Cross; so also is it of Grace, elsewhere called Wisdom.

Finally, the Cross regarded from this point of view is called Bread, the substance of Life.

In a remarkable paper in *The Theosophical Review*, Nov., 1907, E. R. Innes speaks of a vision of a great drama of those Powers beyond the mind-spheres, which in the Indian scriptures are called Food and Eater—that is to say, the mystical union between the Not-self and the Self.

In the *Chhāndogyopaniṣhad*, for instance, we read of one who had passed into the heaven-world possessing a knowledge of the identity of the Self and Not-self. The transformations of his vehicles that thus occur in the inner states or worlds become as it were processes of natural digestion in his Great Body, for we read:

"Having what food he wills, what form he wills, this song he singing sits:

"'O wonder, wonder, wonder!
Food I; food I; food I!
Food-eater I; food-eater I; food-eater I!'"[3]

Our author in similar fashion writes of a soul watching the processes of its own substance in the heaven-world.

"She watched the interaction of those two great currents of the One Great Life-Force—the Life-Force as Supporter, the Life-Force as Sustainer. She watched the great transfiguration of the crossing over of the surface-forms as life met life in perfect mystic union. As the currents crossed the forms changed, but without loss of life or consciousness. The Powers crossed and recrossed; and with each appearance of that sacred symbol there was further expansion and intensification of the Life-Force. At each piercing or insinuation of the one into the other, that which had been two became one, yet there still remained the two. She watched the great mystery of that Cross on which the Heavenly Man dies in order to live again.

"In heaven you do not demolish forms in order to sustain life, you daily insinuate yourself into all the forms you meet, and thus by supplying them with food, the food of your own greater life, you become each separate object, and gain in power and expansiveness. Thus in heaven by sacrifice do you grow and live, and slowly become the world. Thus in heaven do you give life to others in order to live yourself; thus do the many

---

[3] See my *World-Mystery*, 2nd ed., p. 179.

rebecome the One. The Great Mystery of the Bread of Life which must be partaken of by all before the Day of Triumph was acted out before her eyes."

And it might be added that as heaven is a state and not a place, the mystery can be consummated on earth, and that this is the true sacrifice of the Christ and the Way to become a Christ.

9. Ideas of this or a similar order may be held not rashly to underlie the words of our text. The Cross of Life may well be called the Harmony—or articulation, or joining-together—of Wisdom, for it is by means of Wisdom that all the contraries are joined together, and this Articulation constitutes the "firm necessity" of Fate, which was also called in the Gnostic schools the Harmony. And if it is a Cross of Life, it is also a Cross of Light, for Life and Light are the eternally united twin-natures, female and male, of the Logos, the Good. Life is Passion and Light is Understanding. The Logos divides Himself to experience and know Himself.

10. All opposites unite in Wisdom as a ground; she is the pure substance in which all the powers play. It is only when the Cross is regarded as a separator, that it may be said to have a right and a left, with good forces on the one hand and evil on the other. The forces are in reality in themselves the same forces; it is the personality of the man (represented by the upright of the Cross), which refers all things to its incomplete self, that regards them as good and evil.

This personality is rooted in the Lower Root or lower nature, and stretches upward towards the Above.

But in reality there are roots above and branches below, or roots below and branches above, of the trunk of this Tree of Life and Light. Though the nomenclature is somewhat different, I cannot refrain from quoting a striking passage from a Gnostic scripture to give the reader some idea of the lofty region of thought to which the Gnosis accustomed its disciples.

It is taken from *The Great Announcement,* a document ascribed by Hippolytus to the very beginning of the Christianized Gnosis. Strong efforts have been made to question this ascription, and to prove the document to be of a later date, but I think I have established a high probability that it may be even a pre-Christian writing[4].

The text is to be found in Hippolytus' *Refutation of all Heresies*[5]:

"To you, therefore, I say what I say and write what I write. And the writing is this:

"Of the universal Æons (Eternities) there are two Branchings, without beginning or end, from one Root, which is the Power unseeable, incomprehensible Silence.

---

[4] see *H.,* i. 184
[5] vi., 18

"Of these Branchings one is manifested from Above—the Great Power, Mind of the universals, ordering all things, male; and the other from Below—Great Thought, female, generating all things.

"Thence partnering one another they pair (lit. have union—*syzygía*), and bring into manifestation the Middle Distance, incomprehensible Air without beginning or end.

"In this is that Father, who supports and nourishes the things which have beginning and end.

"This is He who has stood, stands and shall stand—a male-female Power in accordance with the transcendent Boundless Power, which hath neither beginning nor end, subsisting in onlyness.

"It was by emanating from this Power (*sci.,* Incomprehensible Silence) that Thought-in-onlyness became two.

"Yet was He, (the Supernal Father) one; for having her (*sci.* Thought) in Himself He was alone [that is, all-one, or only, that is one-ly]. He was not, however, [in this state] 'first,' although transcendent; it was only in manifesting Himself from Himself that He became 'second' [that is to say, as He who stands]. Nay, He was not even called 'Father' till Thought named Him 'Father.'

"As, therefore, Himself pro-ducing Himself by means of Himself, He manifested to Himself His own Thought; so also His Thought on manifesting did not make [Him], but beholding Him, she concealed the Father, that is the Power, in Herself, and is [thus] male-female, Power and Thought.

"Thence is it that they partner one another (for Power in no way differs from Thought) and yet are one. From the things Above is discovered Power, and from those Below Thought.

"So is it, too, with that which is manifested from them; namely, that though it (*sci.* the Middle Distance, Incomprehensible Air) is one, it is found to be two, male-female, having the female in itself.

"Thus is Mind in Thought—inseparable from one another, which though one are yet found to be two."

I believe that our Vision of the Cross sets forth in living symbol precisely what is explained above in more "abstract" terms. It would, however, be a mistake to make abstractions of these sublime ideas; they must be realized as fullnesses, as transcendent realities. The Air, the Batos, the Middle Distance, is the manifestation, or thinking-manifest, of the Divine to Itself, the true meaning of *mā-yā.* [6]

---

[6] See the Trismegistic Sermon, "Though Unmanifest God is most Manifest," and the commentary, *H.,* ii., 99-109

11. I have translated the term διαπηξάμενος by "cross-beaming," for διαπήγιον is a "cross-beam"; and I would refer the reader to the famous myth of Plato known as "The Vision of Er," where the same idea is set forth when we read:

"There they saw the extremities of the Boundaries of the Heaven, extended in the midst of the Light; for this Light was the final Boundary of Heaven—*somewhat like the undergirdings of ships*—and thus confined its whole revolution."[7]

This "cross-beaming" or operation of the Cross is the mode of the energizing of the Logos. It is the simultaneous separating and joining of the generable and the ingenerable, the two modes of the Self-generable; it is the link between personal and impersonal, bound and free, finite and infinite. It is the instrument of creation, male-female in one.

12. There is little surprise, therefore, in learning that this mystery is not the "cross of wood" which the disciple will see and has seen in the pictures framed by his lower mind, when reading the historicized narrative of the mystery-drama or hearing the great story. Nor is it to be imagined that the Lord could be hung upon such a cross of wood, seeing that He is crucified in all men—He whom even the disciple in contemplation cannot see as He is, but can only hear the Wisdom of His Voice.

---

[7] See *H.,* i., 440.

13. "I was held to be what I am not." As to what the many say concerning the mystery, they speak as the many vain and contradictory opinions. Nay, even those who believed in Him have not understood; they have been content with a poor and unworthy conception of the mystery.

The teaching seems to be that as the Christ-story was intended to be the setting-forth of an exemplar of what perfected man might be—namely, that the path was fully opened for him all the way up to God—it was spiritual suicide to rest content with a limited and prejudiced view. Every mould of thought was to be broken, every imperfect conception was to be transcended, if there was to be realization.

For those who cling to the outward forms and symbols the Place of Rest is neither seen nor spoken of. This Place of Rest, this Home of Peace, is in reality the very Cross itself, the Firm Foundation, the that on which the whole creation rests. And if the Place of Rest, where all things cross, and unite, the Mystic Centre of the whole system, which is everywhere, is not seen or spoken of, "much more shall the Lord of it be neither seen nor spoken of"—He who has the power, of the Centre, who can adjust His "centre of gravity" at every moment of time, and therewith the attitude of this Great Body or, if it be preferred, of his Mind, and thus be in perpetual balance, as the Justified and the Just One.

14. The interpretation of the Vision that follows in the text may in its turn be interpreted from several standpoints. It may be regarded cosmicly according to the *restauratio omnium*, when the whole creation becomes the object of the Great Mercy, as Basilides calls it; or it may be taken soteriologically as referring to the salvation or the making safe or sure of our humanity, or it may be referred to the perfection of the individual man.

The multitude of one appearance are the Earth-bound, the Hylics as the Gnostics called them; that is, those who are immersed in things of matter, the "delights of the world." They are the Dead, because they are under the sway of birth-and-death, the spheres of Fate. They have not yet "risen from the Dead," and consciously ascended the Cross of Light and Life.

Thus in the preface to *The Book of the Gnoses of the Invisible God*, that is to say, "The Book of the Gnosis of Jesus the Living One"—which begins with the beautiful words: "I have loved you and longed to give you Life"—we read the following Saying of the Lord:

"Jesus saith: Blessed is the man who crucifieth the world, and doth not let the world crucify him."

And later on the mystery is set forth in another Saying:

"Jesus saith: Blessed is the man who knoweth this Word, and hath brought down the Heaven, and borne the Earth and raised it heavenwards; and he becometh the Midst, for it (the Midst) is a 'nothing.'"[8]

Those who have become spiritual, who have "risen from the Dead," are born into the Race of the Logos, they become kin with Him.

Of this Race much has been written by the mystics of the many different schools of these early days.

Thus the Jewish Gnostic commentator of the Naassene Document writes:

"One is the Nature Below which is subject to Death; and one is the Race without a king [that is, those who are kings of themselves] which is born Above"[9].

And the Christian Gnostic commentator refers to the "ineffable Race of perfect men"[10], who are in the Logos.

Such *illuminati* were called by one tradition of the Christianized Gnosis the Race of Elxai, the Hidden Power or Holy Spirit, the Spouse of Iexai, the Hidden Lord or Logos. [11]

Philo of Alexandria tells us that "Wisdom, who, after the fashion of a mother, brings forth the self-taught

---

[8] *F.*, 518, 519.

[9] *H.*, i., 164.

[10] *H.*, i., 166

[11] *H.*, ii., 242; see my *Did Jesus live 100 B.C.?* chap. xviii.

Race, declares that God is the Sower of it"[12]. This is the term he applies to his beloved Therapeuts, adding that "this Race is rare and found with difficulty."

Elsewhere he tells us that the angels are the "people" of God; but there is a still higher degree of union, whereby a man becomes one of the Race, or Kin, of God. This Race is an intimate union of all them who are "kin to Him"; they become one. For this Race "is one, the highest one; but 'people' is the name of many."

"As many, then, as have advanced in discipline and instruction, and been perfected therein, have their lot among this 'many.'

"But they who have passed beyond these introductory exercises, becoming natural disciples of God, receiving Wisdom free from all toil, migrate to this incorruptible and perfect Race, receiving a lot superior to their former lives in genesis"[13].

And so in one of the Hymns of Thrice Greatest Hermes, after the triple trisagion, the "Hermes" or Illuminated prays:

---

[12] *H.,* i., 220
[13] *H.,* i., 554.

"And fill me with Thy Power and with this Grace of Thine, that I may give the Light to those in ignorance of the Race—my Brethren and Thy Sons."[14]

Philo calls it "self-taught," just as the Buddhists speak of the Arhats as *asekha*; and the Trismegistic teacher writes:

"This Race, my sons, is never taught; but when He willeth it, its memory is restored by God."[15]

The "Elect Race" of Valentinus is the "Sonship" of Basilides that incarnates on earth for the abolition of Death. [16]

In the *Pistis Sophia* document, the Sophia, or the soul turning towards the Light, first utters seven repentances, or "turnings-of-the-mind," or rather of the whole nature. At the fourth of these, the turning-point of some subcycle of the great Return, she prays that the Image of the Light may not be turned or averted from her, for the time is come when "those who turn in the lowest regions" should be regarded—"the mystery which is made the type of the Race."[17]

Again in the introduction to *The Book of the Great Logos according to the Mystery*, the disciples beg the

---

[14] *H.,* ii., 20.
[15] *H.,* ii., 221.
[16] *F.,* 303.
[17] *F.,* 471.

Master to explain the Mystery of the Word. Jesus answers that the Life of His Father consists in their purifying their souls from all earthly stain, and making them to become the Race of the Mind, so that they may be filled with understanding and by His teaching perfect themselves.[18]

Finally in the marvellous *Untitled Apocalypse* of the Bruce Codex we read:

"These words said the Lord of the Universe to them, and disappeared from them, and hid Himself from them.

"And the Births-of-matter rejoiced that they had been remembered, and were glad that they had come out of the narrow and difficult place, and prayed to the Hidden Mystery:

"'Give us authority that we may create for ourselves æons and worlds according to Thy Word, upon which Thou didst agree with Thy servant; for Thou alone art the changeless One, Thou alone the boundless, the uncontainable, self-taught, self-born Self-father; Thou alone art the unshakeable and unknowable; Thou alone art Silence and Love, and Source of all; Thou alone art virgin of matter, spotless; whose Race no man can tell, whose manifestation no man can comprehend.'"[19]

---

[18] *F.*, 528.
[19] *F.*, 564.

To understand, man must pass beyond the stage of man, and self-realize himself as "kin to Him"—the Logos.

It is, however, doubtful whether "Race" is the correct reading in our text; but as it is the clear reading in 15 the above notes are germane to our study. The MS. apparently reads "every Limb." This again is one of the most general Gnostic mystical terms, and is taken over from the Osiric Mysteries. The Limbs of the God are scattered abroad, and collected together again in the resurrection. The inner meaning of this graphic symbolism may be gleaned from the following striking passages.

In a MS. of the Gnostic Marcus there is a description of the method of symbolizing the Great Body of the Heavenly Man, whereby the twenty-four letters of the Greek alphabet were assigned in pairs to the twelve Limbs. This Body was the symbol of the ideal economy, dispensation or ordering of the universe, its planes, regions, hierarchies, and powers.[20]

This also is the true Body of man, the Source of all his bodies. And so we read the following mystery-saying in *The Gospel of Eve*:

"I stood on a lofty mountain and saw a Great Man, and another, a dwarf, and heard as it were a Voice of thunder, and drew nigh for to hear. And He spake unto me and said: 'I am thou, and thou art I; and wheresoever

---

[20] *F.*, 366.

thou art, I am there, and in all am I sown (or scattered).
And whencesoever thou willest, thou gatherest Me; and
gathering Me, thou gatherest Thyself."[21]

This is a vision of the Great Person and little person, of
the Higher Self and lower self. It may also be
interpreted in terms of the Logos and humanity; but it
comes nearer home to think of it as the mystery of the
individual man—the scattering of the Limbs of the
Great Person in the personalities that have been his in
many births.

This idea is brought out more clearly in a passage from
The Gospel of Philip. It is an apology or defence, as it
was called, a formula to be used by the soul in its ascent
above, as it passed through the space of the Midst; and
for the mystic it is a declaration of the state of a man
who is in his last compulsory earth-life.

"I have recognised myself, and gathered myself together
from all sides. I have sown no children for the Ruler,
but have torn up his roots, and have gathered together
my Limbs that were scattered abroad. I know Thee who
Thou art; for I am of those from Above."[22]

He has sown no children to the Ruler, the Lord of
Death; he has not contracted any fresh debt, or created a
new form of personality, into which he must again
incarnate. But he has torn up the roots of Death, by

---

[21] *F.*, 439.
[22] *Ibid.*

shattering the form of egoity, and bursting the bonds of Fate. He has gathered together his Limbs, completed the articulation of his Perfect Body.

The Limbs were according to certain orderings, one of which was the configuration of the five-fold Star, the five-limbed Man. Thus in *The Acts of Thomas* we read:

"Come Thou who art more ancient far than the five holy Limbs—Mind, Thought, Reflection, Thinking, Reasoning! Commune with them of later birth!"[23]

These five Limbs are also the five Words of the mystery of the Vesture of Light in the *Pistis Sophia* , with which the Christ is clothed in power on the Day of Triumph, the Great Day "Come unto us," when His Limbs are gathered together and the Song of the Powers begins:

"Come unto us, for we are Thy Fellow-Limbs. We are all one with thee. We are one and the same, and Thou art one and the same."

In the whole document much is said of the "sweet mysteries that are in the Limbs of the Ineffable," but it would be too long to repeat it here. It will be perhaps of greater service to append a very striking passage, from *The Books of the Saviour,* which has been copied into the MS. of the *Pistis Sophia* :

---

[23] *F.,* 422.

"And they who are worthy of the Mysteries that dwell in the Ineffable, which are those that have not emanated—these are prior to the First Mystery. To use a similitude and correspondence of speech that ye may understand, they are the Limbs of the Ineffable. And each is according to the dignity of its Glory—the Head according to the dignity of the Head, the Eye according to the dignity of the Eye, the Ear according to the dignity of the Ear, and the rest of the Limbs [in like fashion]; so that the matter is plain: There are many Limbs (Members) but only one Body.

"Of this I have spoken in a plan, a correspondence and similitude, but not in its true form; nor have I revealed the Word in Truth, but as the Mystery of the Ineffable.

"And all the Limbs that are in Him..., that is, they that dwell in the Mystery of the Ineffable, and they that dwell in Him, and also the Three Spaces that follow according to their Mysteries—of all of these in truth and verity am I the Treasure; apart from which there is no Treasure peculiar to [this] cosmos. But there are other Words and Mysteries and Regions [of other worlds].

"Now, therefore, Blessed is he who hath found the Words of the Mysteries of the Space towards the exterior. He is a God who hath found the Words of the Mysteries of the second Space, in the midst. He is a Saviour and free of every space who hath found the

Words of the Mysteries of the third Space towards the interior....

"But He, on the other hand, who hath found the Words of the Mysteries which I have set forth for you according to a similitude—namely, the Limbs of the Ineffable—Amēn I say unto you, that man who hath found the Words of those Mysteries in the Truth of God, he is the First in Truth, and like unto Him; for it is through these Words and Mysteries that [all things are made] and the universe itself stands through that First One. Therefore is he who hath found the Words of these Mysteries, like unto the First. For it is the gnosis of the Gnosis of the Ineffable in which I have spoken with you this day."

It is thus seen that the means used in revealing the manner of the highest Mysteries of the Ineffable was by the similitude of the Limbs or Members of the Body. It, therefore, follows, as we have already seen, that this symbolism was one of the most, if not the most, fundamental in this Gnosis. The three stages of perfectioning are those of the Saint, God and Saviour. But these are still stages in evolution or process, no matter how sublime they be. The fourth or consummation is other; it transcends process, it is ever itself with itself, embracing all processes and all powers simultaneously. But we must not be tempted to comment on this instructive passage, for there is quite enough material in it to develop into a small treatise in itself. For an admirable intuition of the Mystery of the

Limbs of the Ineffable, and the meaning of the words "the Head is according to the dignity of the Head," etc., the reader is referred to the beautiful passage in *The Untitled Apocalypse* of the Bruce Codex, quoted in the comments on *The Hymn of Jesus* .

The Gnostic seers lost themselves in the contemplation of the simultaneous simplicity and multiplicity of these Mysteries. Thus again in the same *Untitled Apocalypse* we read:

"He it is whose Limbs (Members) make a myriad of myriads of Powers, each one of which comes from Him."[24].

This graphic symbolism of the Limbs is derived from the tradition of the Osiric Mysteries. Many a passage could be quoted in illustration from *The Book of the Coming-forth by Day,* that strange and marvellous collection of Egyptian Rituals commonly known as the *Book of the Dead;* but perhaps the under-meaning of the mystery is nowhere more clearly shown than in the following magnificent passage from *The Litany of the Sun,* inscribed on the Tombs of the Kings of ancient Thebes:

"The Kingly Osiris is an intelligent Essence. His Limbs conduct Him; His 'Fleshes' open the way for Him. Those who are born from Him create Him. They rest when they have caused the Kingly Osiris to be born.

---

[24] *F.,* 547

"It is He who causes them to be born. It is He who engenders them. It is He who causes them to exist. His Birth is the Birth of Rā in Amenti. He causes the Kingly Osiris to be born; He causes the Birth of Himself."[25]

It requires no elaboration to show that this is precisely the same mystery as the secret set forth in our Vision of the Cross. The Kingly Osiris is Ātman, the Self, the True Man, the Monad. This is the Kingly Osiris in his male-female nature, self-creative. Ātman is both the producer and product of evolution. In a restricted sense the above may be interpreted from the standpoint of the individuality and its series of personalities in incarnation.

15. And now to return to the text. The Race is the Upper Nature, now scattered abroad in the hearts of men; it is the true Spirit of man, the hidden Divinity within him. It is this which re-turns, and so causes the man to turn or repent. It is obedient, that is audient, to the Voice of the Self, the compelling Utterance of the Logos. He who not only hears, but hearkens to or obeys the sweet counsels of this Great Persuasion, becomes this Upper Nature consciously; and therefore it no longer is what it was, for it is conscious in the man, and so the man is above men of the lower nature.

16. These mysterious sentences all set forth the state of true Self-consciousness. So long as man is not conscious

---

[25] See my *World-Mystery*, 2nd ed., p. 162.

that he is Divine, so long is the Divine in him not what it really is; the "lower" "limits" the "higher." Union is attained by "hearkening," by "attention." Then it is that the man becomes his Higher Self, and that Higher Self becomes in its turn the Self, having taken his self in separation into his Self as union.

17. This "attention" is the straining or striving towards the One; and therefore no attention must be paid to the many. The whole strife of warring opinions and doubts must be reconciled, or at-oned, within the Mystery. The thought must be allowed to dwell but little on "those without." A height must be reached from which the whole human drama can be seen as a spectacle below and within; this height is not with regard to space and place, but with respect to consciousness and realization that all is taking place within the man's Great Body as the operations of the Divine economy. They who are "without the mystery" are not arbitrarily excluded, but are those who prefer to go forth without instead of returning within.

18. They who have re-turned, or turned back on themselves, and entered into themselves for the realization of true Self-consciousness, alone can understand the meaning of the Great Passion, as has been so admirably set forth in the Mystery-Ritual of the Dance.

Those who have consciousness of these spiritual verities, nay, even those who have but dimly felt their greatness, will easily understand that the story of the crucifixion as believed in by the masses was for the Gnostics but the shadow of an eternal happening that most intimately concerned every man in his inmost nature.

19. The outer story was centred round a dramatic crisis of death on a stationary cross—a dead symbol, and a symbol of death. But the inner rite was one of movement and "dancing," a living symbol and a symbol of life. This was shown to the disciple—indeed, as we have seen, he was made in the Dance to partake in it—that he might know the mystery of suffering in a moment of Great Experience. He saw it and became it; it was shown him in action. He had seen sorrow and suffering, and the cause of it had been dimly felt; but its ceasing he did not yet know really, for the ceasing of sorrow could only come when he could realize sorrow and joy, suffering and bliss, simultaneously. And that mystery the Christ alone knows.

20. Let the disciple then first see the suffering of the man through, not his own, but His Master's eyes. He will first only see the mystery, grasp it intellectually; he will not as yet realize it. When he realizes it, there will then be bliss indeed, for he will begin to become the Master Himself. And the Master is the conqueror of woe—not, however, in the sense of the annihilator of it, but as the one who rejoices in it; for he knows that it is the necessary concomitant of bliss, and that the more pain he suffers in one portion of his nature, the more bliss he experiences in another; the deeper the one the

deeper the other, and therewith the intenser becomes his whole nature. His Great Body is learning to respond to greater and greater impulses or "vibrations."

The consummation is that he becomes capable of experiencing joy in sorrow and sorrow in joy; and thus reaches to the gnosis that these are inseparables, and that the solution of the mystery is the power of ever experiencing both simultaneously.

21. It may thus to some extent become clear that what is asserted of the Christ in the general Gospel-story is typically true and yet is not true. Those who look at one side only of the living picture see in a glass darkly.

If we could only realize that all the ugliness and misery and confusion of life is but the underside, as it were, of a pattern woven on the Great Loom or embroidered by Divine Fingers! We can in our imperfect consciousness see only the underside, the medley of crossing of threads, the knots and finishings-off; we cannot see the pattern. Nevertheless it exists simultaneously with the underside. The Christ sees both sides simultaneously, and understands.

22. But the term that our Gnostic writer chooses with which to depict this grade of being is not Christ, but Word or Reason (Logos). This Reason is not the ratiocinative faculty in man which conditions him as a duality; it is rather more as a Divine Monad, as Pure Reason, or that which can hold all opposites in one. It is

called Word because it is the immediate intelligible Utterance of God.

23. This is the first mystery that man must learn to understand; then will he be able to understand God as unity; and only finally will he understand the greatest mystery of all—man, the personal man, the thing we each of us now are, God in multiplicity, and why there is suffering.

24. With this the writer breaks off, knowing fully how difficult it is to express in human speech the living ideas that have come to birth in him, and knowing that there are still more marvellous truths of which he has caught some glimpse or heard some echo, but which he feels he can in no way set forth in proper decency.

And so he tells us the Lord is taken up, unseen by the multitudes. That is to say, presumably, no one in the state of the multiplicity of the lower nature can behold the vision of unity.

25. When he descends from the height of contemplation, however, he remembers enough to enable him to laugh at the echoes of his former doubts and fancies and misconceptions, and to make him realize the marvellous power of the natural living symbolic language that underlies the words of the mystery-narrative that sets forth the story of the Christ.

POSTCRIPT.

The vision itself is not so marvellous as the instruction; nevertheless it allows us to see that the Cross in its supernal nature is the Heavenly Man with arms outstretched in blessing, showering benefits on all—the perpetual Self-sacrifice[26]. And in this connection we should remind ourselves of the following striking sentence from *The Untitled Apocalypse* of the Bruce Codex, an apocalypse which contains perhaps the most sublime visions that have survived to us from the Gnosis:

"The Outspreading of His Hands is the manifestation of the Cross."

And then follows the key of the mystery:

"The Source of the Cross is the Man [Logos] whom no man can comprehend."[27]

No man can comprehend Man; the little cannot contain the Great, except potentially.

It was some echo of this sublime teaching that found its way into the naïve though allegorical narrative of *The Acts of Philip*. When Philip was crucified he cursed his enemies.

---

[26] *F.*, 330

[27] See *Hymn of Jesus*

"And behold suddenly the abyss was opened, and the whole of the place in which the proconsul was sitting was swallowed up, and the whole of the temple, and the viper which they worshipped, and great crowds, and the priests of the viper, about seven thousand men, besides women and children, except where the apostles were; they remained unshaken."

This is a cataclysm in which the lower nature of the man is engulfed. The apostles are his higher powers; the rest the opposing forces. The latter plunge into Hades and experience the punishments of those who crucify the Christ and his apostles. They are thus converted and sing their repentance. Whereupon a Voice was heard saying: "I shall be merciful to you in the Cross of Light."

Philip is reproved by the Saviour for his unmerciful spirit.

"But I, O Philip, will not endure thee, because thou hast swallowed up the men in the abyss; but behold My Spirit is in them, and I will bring them up from the dead; and thus they, seeing thee, shall believe in the Glory of Him that sent thee.

"And the Saviour having turned, stretched up His hand, and marked a Cross in the Air coming down from Above even unto the Abyss, and it was full of Light, and had its form after the likeness of a ladder. And all the multitude that had gone down from the City into the Abyss came up on the Ladder of the Cross of Light; but there remained below the proconsul and the viper which these worshipped. And when the multitude had come up, having looked upon Philip hanging head downwards, they lamented with great lamentation at the lawless action which they had done."

The doers of the "lawless" deed are the same as the "lawless Jews" in the *Acts of John*—"those who are under the law of the lawless Serpent"; that is to say, those who are under the sway of Generation, as contrasted with those under the law of Re-generation[28].

Philip stands for the man learning the last lesson of divine mercy. The Proconsul and the Viper are the antitypes of the Saviour and the Serpent of Wisdom. The crucifixion of Philip is, however, not the same as the crucifixion of the Christ; he is hanged reversed, his head to the earth and not towards heaven. It is a lower grade of the mysteries.

Concerning the mystery of the crucifixion of the Christ we learn somewhat of its inner nature from the doctrines of the Docetæ.

His baptism was on this wise: He washed Himself in the Jordan, that is the Stream of the Logos, and after His purification in the Life-giving Water, He became possessed of a spiritual or perfect body, the type and signature of which were in accordance with the matter of his virginity, that is of virgin substance; so that when

---

[28] see *Hymn of Jesus*, pp. 28, 47

the World-ruler, or God of generation or death, condemned his own plasm, the physical body, to death, that is to the Cross, the soul nourished in that physical body might strip off the body of flesh, and nail it to the "tree," and yet triumph over the powers of the Ruler and not be found naked, but clothed in a robe of glory. Hence the saying: "Except a man be born of Water and the Spirit he cannot enter into the Kingship of the Heavens; that which is born of the flesh is flesh."[29]

It was because of these and such like ideas, and in the conviction that the mystery of the crucifixion was to be worked out in every man, that a Gnostic writer, following the Valentinian tradition, explains a famous passage in the Pauline *Letter to the Ephesians* as follows:

"'For this cause I bow my knees to the God and Father and Lord of our Lord Jesus Christ, that God may vouchsafe to you that Christ may dwell in your inner man'—that is to say, the psychic and not the bodily man—'that ye may be strong to know what is the Depth'—that is, the Father of the universals—'and what is the Breadth'—that is the Cross, the Boundary of the Plērōma [or Fullness]—'and what is the Greatness'— that is, the Plērōma of the æons [the eternities or universals, the Limbs of the Body of the Ineffable]."[30]

---

[29] *F.*, p. 221
[30] *F.*, 532

To be closely compared with the Vision in *The Acts of John* is the Address of Andrew to the Cross in *The Acts of Andrew*. They both plainly belong to the same tradition, and might indeed have been written by the same hand.

"Rejoicing I come to thee, Thou Cross, the Life-giver, Cross whom I now know to be mine. I know thy mystery; for thou hast been planted in the world to make-fast things unstable.

"Thy head stretcheth up into heaven, that thou mayest symbol-forth the Heavenly Logos, the Head of all things.

"Thy middle parts are stretched forth, as it were hands to right and left, to put to flight the envious and hostile power of the Evil One, that thou mayest gather together into one them [*sci.*, the Limbs] that are scattered abroad.

"Thy foot is set in the earth, sunk in the deep [*i.e.*, abyss], that thou mayest draw up those that lie beneath the earth and are held fast in the regions beneath it, and mayest join them to those in heaven.

"O Cross, engine, most skilfully devised, of Salvation, given unto men by the Highest; O Cross, invincible trophy of the Conquest of Christ o'er His foes; O Cross, thou life-giving tree, roots planted on earth, fruit treasured in heaven; O Cross most venerable, sweet thing and sweet name; O Cross most worshipful, who bearest as grapes the Master, the true vine, who dost bear, too, the Thief as thy fruit, fruitage of faith through confession; thou who bringest the worthy to God through the Gnosis and summonest sinners home through repentance!"

A magnificent address indeed. The identification of the Master and the man with the Cross and in the Cross is hardly disguised. The Cross is the Tree of Life and the tree of death simultaneously. "Give up thy life that thou mayest live," says that inspired mystic treatise, *The Voice of the Silence*, and this is no other than the secret of the Mystery of the Cross. The Master is hanged between two thieves, the one repentant and the other obdurate, the soul turned towards the Light and towards the Darkness, all united in the one Mystery of the Cross—the Mystery of Man.

We have seen above that Philip is hanged head downwards, but he is not the most famous instance of this reversal. The best known is associated with the name of Peter in the mystic romances.

Thus in a fragment of the Linus-collection called *The Martyrdom of Peter*, we learn the doctrine as set forth in a speech put into the mouth of Peter thus crucified:

"Fitly wast Thou alone stretched on the Cross with head on high, O Lord, who hast redeemed all of the world from sin.

"I have desired to imitate Thee in Thy Passion too; yet would I not take on myself to be hanged upright.

"For we, pure men and sinners, are born from Adam, but Thou art God of God, Light of true Light, before all æons and after them; thought worthy to become for men Man without strain of man, Thou has stood forth man's glorious Saviour—Thou ever upright, ever raised on high, eternally Above!

"We, men according to the flesh, are sons of the First Man (Adam), who sank his being in the earth, whose fall in human generation is shown forth.

"For we are brought to birth in such a way, that we do seem to be poured into earth, so that the right is left, the left doth right become; in that our state is changed in those who are the authors of this life.

"For this world down below doth think the right what is the left—this world in which Thou, Lord, hast found us like the Ninevites, and by Thy holy preaching hast thou rescued these about to die."

The "authors of this life" of reversal, are the "parents" of the "lower nature"; not our natural parents whom we are to love, but the powers of illusion we are to abandon. The Jonah-myth was used as a type of the Initiate, who after being "three days" in the Belly of the Fish, the Great Life or Animal that dwells in the Ocean or Great Water, is vomited forth re-generate, and so a fit vehicle for preaching with compelling words or acts for the benefit of those in Nineveh or the Jerusalem Below, or this world.

But for those who had ears to hear there was a still further instruction concerning the secret of the Mystic Cross.

"But ye, my brothers, who have the right to hear, lend me the ears of your heart, and understand what now must be revealed to you—the hidden mystery of every nature and secret source of every thing composed.

"For the First Man, whose race I represent by my position, with head reversed, doth symbolize the birth into destruction; for that his birth was death and lacked the Life-stream.

"But of His own compassion the Power Above came down into the world, by means of corporal substance, to him who by a just decree had been cast down into the earth, and hanged upon the Cross, and by the means of this most holy calling [the Cross] He did restore us, and did make for us these present things (which had till then remained unchanged by men's unrighteous error) into the Left, and those that men had taken for the Left into eternal things.

"In exaltation of the Right He hath changed all the signs into their proper nature, considering as good those thought not good, and those men thought malefic most benign.

"Whence in a mystery the Lord hath said: 'If ye make not the Right like to the Left, the Left like to the Right,

Above as the Below, Before as the Behind, ye shall not know God's Kingdom.'"[31]

"This saying have I made manifest in myself, my brothers; this is the way in which your eyes of flesh behold me hanging. It figures forth the Way of the First Man.

"But ye, beloved, hearing these words, and, by conversion of your nature and changing of your life, perfecting them, even as ye have turned you from that Way of Error where ye trod, unto the most sure state of Faith, so keep ye running, and strive towards the Peace that calls you from Above, living the holy life. For that the Way in which ye travel there is Christ.

"Therefore with Jesus, Christ, true God, ascend the Cross. He hath been made for us the One and Only Word; whence also doth the Spirit say: 'Christ is the Word and Voice of God.'

"The Word in truth is symbolled forth by that straight stem on which I hang. As for the Voice—since that voice is a thing of flesh, with features not to be ascribed unto God's nature, the cross-piece of the Cross is thought to figure forth that human nature which suffered the fault of change in the First Man, but by the help of God-and-man received again its real Mind.

---

[31] This saying is from *The Gospel according to the Egyptians*.

"Right in the centre, joining twain in one, is set the nail of discipline—conversion and repentance."[32]

The interpretation becomes somewhat strained towards the end. The reversed hanging typified the man of sex, or the man still under the sway of generation, separated into male and female. Such hang head-downwards in the Great Womb of Nature, and all is reversed for them. Hanged upright, the re-generate man contains in himself in active operation the twin powers in union, now used for spiritual creation, and self-perfection.

And if it be thought that there is abandonment of any thing in this consummation, then let it be known that it is only a giving up of the part for the whole, the passing from the state of separation to the realization of inexpressible bliss; for as the inspired writer of *The Untitled Apocalypse* phrases it in an ecstasy of enthusiasm:

"This is the eternal Father; this the ineffable, unthinkable, incomprehensible, untranscendible Father. He it is in whom the All became joyous; it rejoiced and was joyful, and brought forth in its joy myriads of myriads of Æons; they were called the 'Births of Joy,' because the All had joyed with the Father.

"These are the worlds from which the Cross upsprang; out of these incorporeal Members did the Man arise."[33]

---

[32] *F.*, 446-449.

[33] *F.*, 550

www.ingramcontent.com/pod-product-compliance
Lightning Source LLC
Chambersburg PA
CBHW071126260626
47162CB00006B/2471